If I were famous, you'd read this

Melaniè

authorHOUSE®

AuthorHouse™
1663 Liberty Drive
Bloomington, IN 47403
www.authorhouse.com
Phone: 833-262-8899

Published by AuthorHouse 08/25/2022

ISBN: 978-1-6655-6364-2 (sc)
ISBN: 978-1-6655-6362-8 (hc)
ISBN: 978-1-6655-6363-5 (e)

Library of Congress Control Number: 2022911834

Print information available on the last page.

"Like a mermaid, her laughter can be a form of imagination, like one who dreams."

–Melanie

"I would rather be loathed for something that I am,
than be loved for something I am not."

–Melanie

"God put eyes in front of our face to always guide us to go forward in life not backwards."

–Melanie

"The mistakes of today are forgotten tomorrow."

–Melanie

"A tragedy, in time, can become a form of laughter."

–Melanie

Contents

"But a mermaid has no tears, and therefore she suffers so much more."

–Hans Christian Anderson

I would like to dedicate this book in memory of my genuine friend Caroline Galm and her husband Willie. She was a petite elderly woman who I met on a cruise and she changed my life. She is the reason why I wanted to work with the elderly. May she rest in peace. And to my brother Chuck who left this world way too soon due to suicide. You had so much potential. I love you, may you rest in peace.

"I would rather be loathed for something that I am,
than be loved for something I am not."

–Melanie

"One person's tragedy is another persons comedy."

–Carol Burnett

"The mistakes of today are forgotten tomorrow."

–Melanie

"Naive Girl"

Naive girl open your eyes
Naive girl do not disguise
See them for who they really are
See through them: you won't go far
Naive girl I said once before
Naive girl you don't ask for more
There's a connection to the choices you made
Naive girl you won't degrade
How could I be so naive?
I see only the good in people
They want to leave
Others will stay till you reach for
The stars
You can reach up high you will go very far
Naive girl you learned a lesson
Naive girl it became an obsession
Naive girl let there be no regret
Naive girl you will repent

"Blurry Glasses"

I'm looking though my glasses
They are quite blurred
I see it, I don't say a word
Can you hear me?
I'm making a fuss
It's not fair; it's I'm just
Little by little I'm falling apart
Blurry glasses
It's from my heart
Blurry glasses you now seemed quite clear
Years of healing, there's nothing to fear
Blurry glasses - give me advice
I see clearly now that I might
Ignore it I'll walk away
But these feelings stay here
Each and everyday
Dirty glasses; I no longer fear
My glasses now that they are clear

"Happy Cries, Happy Problems"

I'm so happy- Can you hear me cry
Do not tempt me I'll tell you why
Your drug I've never tried
My guides tell me that I would die
So I sing these words from long ago
Looking back its what I do know
What I've learned; how so profound
Like it was lost
Now it is found
Hey! Do you feel like you're all alone
Keep it private it's what I have known
The colors shine like a bright rainbow
Is it a deer, a friend or a foe?
My goodness! Don't give into the shame
For you know, it was part of a game
For now I won't try to ignore
The visions, the vibration
A profound lure

"Ying and Yang"

Ying and Yang
There is darkness within light
There is light within darkness
All that I might
That I will harness
Live all alone for your small sorrow
I'll live all alone - I will not borrow
To think about what I truly need
A token of love
It starts with a seed
So I ask you what do you need now
It's so hard to release
I'll show you how
Beware although it will be transmuted
A dove, a symbol to be muted
A positive vibe all in your aura
I will regress; there will be no sorrow

"You Deserve It"

It's hard to stand up for yourself
When you are deeply wounded and shamed
They will intimidate
Life can be a game
Don't be set back
Learn to take a chance
Stand up for yourself
You can take a stance
A glass half full
You think: Why am I here?
You can evolve your soul
You will feel very near
Of all the things I've gone through
I think of you the most
You struggled in your career
Now lets take a toast
Thank you from my heart you make it
Very clear - Success and abundance
They are very near

"Gay Men and Chocolate"

It's hard to stand up for yourself
Especially when you are deeply
Wounded and burn
You'll shake you'll cough
You'll want to learn
To say clearly there's two things
In life I like the best:
Gay men and chocolate
Your life is not a test
Gay men and chocolate
I do not melt
There's no attraction
But I'm still svelt
I love you and
You tell me I am beautiful
Gay men and chocolate
It's quite lackadaisical
Gay men and chocolate
I know your path is a tough one
A holy graft
you may feel like your the only one
Until you come out of the closet they say
Don't be alone
you will not feel shame
If you could be gay
A star— you could be well known
Gay men and chocolate
I hope you're not alone
Gay men and chocolate
Gay men and chocolate
You can call me home
You're not alone
Gay men and chocolate
You are not alone

"A Reflection of the Past"

I was totally wrong
But I told the truth
I'm shaking like a chicken
When it hurts the most
It's so painful
People are so mean
You can't expect them not to judge me
It's a scary dream
Now I tell you
The years that have gone by
All alone I've spent
I try, I do try
Healing and evolving again
To evolve my soul
Please, if you wish, I beg your pardon
The truth will be told

"Behind the Scenes"

I see the other side of the story
I was totally wrong
It's not right
Now I sing this song
Sin separates us from God
It's not right
You can rise above it
I know that I might
Take a piece of glory, clearing up my karma
What I did, right and wrong
All of this drama
Genuine people get screwed over from the dark
Left and right
I resent it
You can get strong and fight
They make you strong
Like I said before
You'll see the pink light
Twinkle even more
It's like a big bright treasure chest
Open it up till you take a rest

"The Big Secret"

There's a secret I need to tell
But I learned; I know it very well
I, many times, do I need
To tell my story?
My guide tell me I should not worry
I, many times, do I need
To tell my story?
My guides tell me
I should not worry
I have been greatly
Stabbed in the back
I will tell you- I'll be exact
It's been many years; there's a secret
I need to tell
But I learned
I know it very well
I have been greatly stabbed in the back
I will tell you, I'll be exact
There's a secret I need to tell
But I learned; I know it very well
I, many times, do I need to
Tell my story?
My guides hold up high
All of my glory
My guides tell me
I should not worry
I, many times
Do I need to tell my story?
In the end, my guides hold up
High, all of my glory

"Forced Into Fame"

I was forced into fame
In this life a real game
It's all I can handle
A real live scandal
There were rumors that were part true
I'm not going to deny
I think of you
I'm so sorry you thought I lied
I tried and I tried
I tried and I tried
There were curses that turned out
To be blessings
Now that I'm second guessing
Life, it can be like a rebirth
If you ask me how
Longer you search
I was forced into fame
In this real life game
It's all I can handle
A real live scandal
It's all I can handle
A real live scandal

"Honestly I Don't Know What to Say"

When I thought of you the other day
Honestly I don't know what to say
It captured me, your honesty
From long ago till now today
When you think of the past
And what you endure
If it's very lucky forever more
I'll dream again
Till it's all I do
However long it may be
I'll think of you
The sunshine, the moon, around a bay
I'll think of you, of you that way
Honestly I don't know what to say
Honestly I don't know what to say
If I may, I'll see your way
If I may, I'll see your way
In all honesty
In all honesty
I thought of you the other day
I dreamed of you, of what to say
Honestly I don't know what to say
Honestly I don't know what to say
Someday again you'll see that way
Someday again you'll see that way
The sunshine, the moon
Around a bay
Honestly I don't know
What to say
Honestly I don't know
What to say
Honestly - Hey!
If it's I may

"Hope for Tomorrow"

Let the angels guide you
Let them abide you
Think of all your sorrow
And about tomorrow
I see a vision
It's of pink light
I've got so much to give
That I just might
Jump start my engine
That I just might
Because I am forgiven
I can reach heights
Think of your sorrow
And about tomorrow
It's what I have been given
And just what I live in
Think of your sorrow
And about tomorrow
Think of your sorrow
There's hope for tomorrow

"About the Dark"

Don't let the dark knock you down
It's how I survived from this town
If in the past you judged me
Now you can see
I told the truth- do you believe?
The dark it can make you live in sin
When you learn and evolve
You can truly win
The dark it can make you live in sin
When you learn and evolve you can truly win
Do not convert me to be a part of your dark
Let's try right now, we can start
See I became very too proud
But I was wrong
Can you say it loud?
It's ok, it was a lesson
Some people call it to vent
Or a confession
I'm so glad
I turned my life around
Change is good- it is so profound

"Two Sides of the Story"

There are both sides of the story
In all of this glory
My honesty may frighten you
Cause I know now what to do
Clearing up my karma
What I did in a past life
Oh how, oh how, I do strife
You see there's a reason for
All of this pain
It's part of the human experience
And how we can gain
Life is all about giving and receiving
And learning how to share
It gives us new meaning
Even when we dare
I am seeing both sides of the story
In all of this glory
Giving and receiving
I'll tell you once again
It is when we will truly win

"Gold Digger"

Gold digger, gold digger dig way deep
Gold digger, gold digger she won't leave
She became your honey
Because you have money
Oh no you're in trouble
Now your life it is a double
Gold digger gold digger
Dig way deep
Gold digger gold digger she won't leave
He found out you were a creep
It's too late now
She became your honey
It's too late now
Because you have money
What a shame; you now must rise above
And everyone thought you were a dove
Gold digger, gold digger dig way deep
It's too late to do anything
About it now she won't leave
Gold digger, gold digger she won't leave.

"Dark Glory"

Don't judge me until you know
My side of the story
Because you won't judge me
In all of my dark glory
I want to change the abuse of power
And the misuse of judgement
I'm trying not to care
But I do care
The shit has hit the fan
I'm trying not to care,
But I do care
The shit has hit the fan
I'm ready to tell my story
In all of my dark glory
I will not worry
I am so damaged
I will not manage
In all of my dark glory
In all of my dark glory
I will not worry
I'll tell my story
I will not worry

"Sing this Song"

Right now I sing this song
But it won't take very long
To show you that
I'm strange because I'm different
I think my behavior was very strange
I was silly and naive
It was a long range
I had to learn to be patient
And not be so impulsive
I'm not going to talk bad about you
But it's all that you do
We say the "f word" when we are angry
And need to release stress
After all said and done
It is a big mess
They say you got to feel it to heal it
Let me tell you
I felt it and it felt really good
And now it is what
I feel that I should do
What's great about healing your life
You can truly change for the better
Clearing up my karma
What I did in the past
This positive energy
It would truly last

"Reliving the Karma"

I would rather be loathed
For something that I am
Than be loved for something I am not
Mistakes: I've made a few
Good karma is what I am due
Many a lives have been hurt
That's why you need to dig in the dirt
Don't ever question your self worth
Sometimes you need to search and search
The dark can convince you
That there is no light
And you try to ignore it
You just might
Step on someone's toes
Will you reach more heights?
Are you forgiven?
I just might
It's what you will live in
You will be forgiven
Maybe you will reach new heights
You just might
Sometimes you need to search and search
The dark can convince you
That there is no light
And you try to ignore it
You just might
It's what you will live in
You will be forgiven
The dark can convince you
That there is no light
Maybe you will reach new heights
I just might
And you try to ignore it

You just might
It's what you will live in
If you will be forgiven
Mistakes: I've made a few
But good karma
Is what I am due

"Undercover the Raw"

Are you a spy? I will try not to hide
But I still try
You have offended me
about a hundred times
Oh my, oh my
How far can I fly?
I can only imagine how far
I can rhyme I will begin again
How far can I fly?
I don't need to prove to you
Or prove to myself that I am gifted
It's over time
my soul it has lifted
I'll take it in cause I am gifted
I know I will truly win, my soul has lifted
You will see
my guides, the pink light
My aura: this has lifted
I'll take it in
Because I am gifted
I will truly win
I do not lie
I will try not to hide
Because I am gifted
But I still try
How far can I fly?
Because I am gifted
my soul it has lifted

"Watch the Game"

I sat back and watched you
Play the game
It's what I deserved
I am full of shame
Wrong and right
Right and wrong
Now I sing this song
The shit has hit the fan
You know I was wrong
In your holy land
It wasn't supposed to happen this way
What do you expect me to say?
It's not right
You don't know what else to say
It wasn't supposed to happen this way
In this holy land
I'm not glad
I stood out from the crowd
I sit back
I now talk really loud
It's not right; the truth you do not know
Are you a friend
I swear you are a foe
So much tragedy the truth you do not know
It wasn't supposed to happen this way
In this holy land
We will grow
Tragedy- it's an opportunity
In this land I know
It will truly be.
In this holy land
We will grow

"Born Again"

I'm a stupid girl
I will try living in this sorrow
I sigh, but there's hope for tomorrow
What I learned from the goddess:
It's an energy
You will grasp it, you will truly see
The thing I don't believe in
Is all of your spells
Because you are manipulating what
They can tell
My religion now is of the Christ
He suffered greatly - I just might
Bow down deeply in form of a prayer
Take that risk if you
Will truly dare
Don't judge me until you know
My side of the story
Then you won't judge me
In all of your glory
I have denounced the devil and
the Illuminati in all of its form
It was a struggle like a great big storm

"It Wasn't Meant To Be"

Eye of the tiger
You are one sly guy
Oh my, oh my
One sly guy, oh my oh my
You could have had me
One sly guy
It's through you I can see
You could have had me
It's through you I can see
One sly guy
I am once more intuitive
It's how I live
I start to sigh
Oh my, oh my
I start to sigh
Oh my, oh my
It's how I live
I had so much to give
You could have had me
It's through you I can see
You are one sly guy
Oh my, oh my
You could have had me
One sly guy
One sly guy
It wasn't meant to be
Together, you and me

"A Different Kind"

My parents put the dollar bill
Before my well being
That's a tough pill to swallow
It's now that I am seeing
Don't call me a role model
I am not perfect
I am very flawed
I am very flawed
It's my well being
It is you I have met
Although you are in awe of me
I won't bow down deep
Till you will truly see
When you speak your mind
You see me
You need to take your time
When you speak your mind
I'll take my time
I'm so different they say
You'd feel the same way
Every other day
You'd feel the same way
If you chose this way
I'm a different kind
I hope you don't mind
I'm a different kind
I'll speak my mind

"Praying For a Miracle"

I was totally wrong
Now I sing this song
I prayed for a miracle
And got one and is
All I care about
Is what is said and done
Until you have none
Life is a mystery
It's how you
Can take those twists and turns
Until you bow down and burn
A reputation that is deeply won
It is said and done
It is said and done
Until you have none
She said "I'm so sorry"
And started to cry
A neighbor, a friend
Afraid to tell me why
A neighbor a friend
She started to cry
A neighbor, a friend
Someday you'll know why
You will cry: A neighbor, a friend
She started to cry
A neighbor a friend
Afraid to tell me why
A neighbor a friend
Someday you'll know why
A neighbor, a friend
You can tell me why
She started to cry

"Angel Recap"

Let the angels guide you
Let the angels abide in you
You've got to feel it to heal it
Let me tell you
I felt it and
It felt really good
I didn't conform in college
I paid the price
I'm trying to make
The uncomfortable people
Feel comfortable
Without being a bullshit artist
I'm very hard on myself
I tell myself
It must be the dark
Everyday I wake up and say
Stay calm
If you are provoked
You made it this far
You made it this far
Don't screw up and give in to the dark
You made it this far
Don't commit a crime
You are sincere
Get it in gear
Let the angels abide in you
You will not fear
Let the angels guide you
Let the angels abide in you

"Confession Booth"

I don't blame Catholicism as a whole
That is not my goal
I am not anti-Catholic but
I blame each priest individually
Who has perpetrated
When these kids grow up they
Feel so hurt
Now they must dig in the dirt
A coverup within the church
Deeper and deeper they all hurt
A deep confession
A priest's evil obsession
Then it sways to purgatory
Karma: what is your story?
It's all about the abuse of power
And who will take down the tower
Forgiving that is the main goal
I am not anti-Catholic
Dig in the dirt
Evolve your soul
I blame each priest
Individually who has perpetrated
A coverup within the church
Deeper and deeper deeper and deeper
They all hurt
A coverup within the church

"Dig Deep"

Dig deep low deeper
Dig way deep
What truth you will keep
Dig deep low deeper
What lies inform you
Dig way deep
Dig way deep
How high will you leap?
Dig deep low deeper
What lies will you keep
Dig deep low deeper
How high can you leap?
Dig deep low deeper
Dig way deep

"Wise to the Game"

To be wise to this game
Of life, it is a journey
there should be no shame
Try not to judge
It's hard not to judge
When one has a past
To relate to them, oh how it lasts
This is what I truly wanted
I've thought of it for years
Somehow it still haunts me
I've shed many tears
When you take a path
That you're really not sure of
Stand in your ground
You will rise above
When you take a path
That you're really not sure of
Be wise to the game
It's hard not to judge
Somehow it still haunts me
That you're really not sure of
Stand in your ground
You will rise above.

"Believe In Yourself"

Believe in yourself
You'll love yourself more of
You see people can be really mean
It must be a thing they're unsure of
They'll talk to you like they really seem
To want to be on your side
But to get off track you'll truly mind
An eclipse, a true vision, a fresh start
You will be born of
So I say this to you do not be naive
Others will see you as one who really seems
The circle of life like someone who
Fell apart
Needed to relax
Begin again to be wise to the game
That you'll start
The circle of life
Like someone who fell apart
An awakening all from my heart
Believe in yourself - last first gasp
Believe in yourself deal with the crap

“Fate”

I fell in love with a rock star
But we didn’t meet at a bar
We “clicked” right away
So I know he will stay
This song is real good luck
It’s funny I don’t feel stuck
I fell in love with a rock star
We “clicked” right away
But we didn’t meet at a bar
So I know he will stay
I’m sure he’s met many a fans
And I’m sure they shook his hands
I’m sure he’s met many a fans
In his gifted land
I fell in love with a rock star
But we didn’t meet at a bar
I fell in love
I fell in love
With a rock star
We didn’t travel very far

I fell in love with a rock star
But we didn't meet at a bar
We clicked right away
So I know he will stay
The sound is real good lord
It's [illegible]
I fell in love with a rock star
We clicked right away
But we didn't meet at a bar
So I know he will stay
[illegible]
And I'm sure the [illegible]
His [illegible]
In his pierced hand
I fell in love with a rock star
But we didn't meet at a bar
I fell in love
I fell in love
With a rock star
We didn't meet at a bar

"Past Life"

I must have done
Something really wrong
In a past life
Cause now I want to hide
It goes over and over in my brain
I think I lost; I will not gain
I think that I'm so hard on myself
Others sympathize waiting
For me to tell
It was quite a struggle
I do try
To continue to live my life
I cannot lie
They say it can be called a scandal
But now I can say
It's all I can handle
I truly want these feelings to go away
But sadly I think that they will stay
I must have done something
Really wrong in a past life
Cause now, surely I want to hide

"Caroline"

She gave me the gift of friendship
In her old age
In a past life she must
Have been on stage
Her star it really shined bright
So I might
Keep in touch; we met on a cruise
A connection- we did not lose
In the disco she danced every night
People thought she was out a sight
Her husband; he didn't travel far
He knew she was a star
In a past life she must have been a star
She traveled very far
She even was legally blind
Did not hold her back
She did not mind
In her old age- alot of lives she
Truly touched
And I miss you, Caroline
I miss you very much

"An Ongoing Test"

You test me to see if
I'll give in
People are sensitive
Don't be so mean
You carry yourself
Oh so confident
In your arena
Of toasted souls
Don't be so mean
You carry yourself
Oh so confident
You test me- will I give in
I am not violent
I won't give in
I am a waste of your time
Please, I will truly win

"A Mixed Emotion"

The winner of the prize
You can no longer survive
As the countdown does count down
We carry ourselves alone in our town
The winner of the prize
Are you a disguise?
You don't seem as how you believe
A mixed emotion is what you seem
A mixed emotion is how you dream
The winner of the prize
You can no longer survive
Are you a disguise?
A mixed emotion is what you seem
A mixed emotion is what you mean
A mixed emotion is how you dream

"The Dead End"

A dead end street
Looking how we will meet
Its closed way around the bend
We wonder how it will amend
I said it a hundred times
Like a clock that does not wind
A dead end street
Looking how we will meet
The street it has an end
We wonder how it will amend
The street- I see the curve
Now clearly you have a nerve
I see clearly there is a surge
A dead end street
Looking how we will meet
A valley; a steep side
I said it a hundred times
Why give in and try to hide
I said it a hundred times

"The Big Lie"

Mommy doesn't know yet
It'll all work out
Honestly, now is the time to "shout"
Someone's lying at my own expense
Mommy doesn't believe me
Once again- I can't vent
They say I am really gifted
But the energy has shifted
Mommy doesn't believe me
Again, I want to leave
The situation: an agrivation
It's stuck up my sleeve
Again, I want to leave
They say everyone has their own story
When mommy finds out, she'll start to worry
And all along it's what I tried to say
Because she found out now she feels
Betrayed

"Sincere"

You have nothing to fear
Because you are sincere
It's all I hear
You have nothing to fear
Oh dear, oh dear
You have nothing to fear
You say, why should I care?
Oh dear, oh dear
Because you are sincere
You have nothing to fear
Where is this going? Where?
I sit there I won't get out of my chair
You have nothing to fear
You say why should I care?
Because you are sincere
Why should I care?
You have nothing to fear
Nothing to fear
Because you are sincere

"Ultimate Betrayal"

Hey! Look! I feel so betrayed
But it looks like it's going to stay
He cheated on me
Now I can see
It's not what it's worth
Like a real birth
You see I start from the beginning
Hope that I'm really winning
Hey! Look I feel so betrayed
But it looks like its going to stay
He cheated on me
Now I can see
It's not what its worth
Like a real birth
Now I can see
Now I can see
He cheated on me
I feel so betrayed
Hey! Look I don't know what to say
Hey! Look I feel so betrayed
But it looks like it's going to stay
Hey! Look I feel so betrayed
Hey! Look I don't know what to say
Hey! Look I feel so betrayed
But it looks like it's going to stay
Hey! Look I feel so betrayed

"Is This Happening?"

I wrote this song
I know you're wrong
I can't believe this is happening
Is this how you truly win?
To take back all that crap
Like driving down a difficult map
I can't believe this is happening
Is this how you truly win?
With what you have sinned
You will take what will be at stake
You'll take a break
Scratch my back
I'll scratch yours
Right on track to devour
I can't believe this is happening
Is this how you truly win?
I wrote this song - you have sinned
I know you're wrong
I can't believe this is happening
I can't believe this is happening
Is this how you truly win?
Once again you have sinned

"What Time Is It?"

I see a clock on the wall
What time will it be when I fall?
They say its a quarter past five
This is true I feel alive
Tick tock tick tock
I see a clock
On the wall
What time will it be when I fall?
This is true I feel alive
This is how I do strive
I never had to lie
I never had to lie
Over and over
I try I try
I never had to lie
I see a clock on the wall
What time will it be when I fall
This is true - I feel alive
This is true - I feel alive
This is true - I feel alive
What time is it?
What time is it?
Too early to say goodbye

"Push Men Away"

I push men away
This is why I stay
It is the ultimate devastation
In this whole wide world nation
So, do you believe in fate?
Or is it destiny that you hate?
To make the uncomfortable person
Feel comfortable
It is what you will
Or just climbing up a hill
How much do you sigh
In all honesty I cannot lie
With the truth until I die
I was in a gutter
Now I can hover
This is why I stay
It's the only way
Hey! Discover a new day
I push men away
This is why I stay
Could it be that they all sin
Oh, do I want to win
With all this hype I want you to be
That people can relate to me
It's how we can see
In all honesty I cannot lie
With the truth until I die

"A Vibe"

Hey! I just got a vibe
I promise you I will not hide
Because that's what good girls
Do or don't do
I have no doubt it's not partially new
If you think that I am weird
Please don't judge me
I'm just really scared
Can't you see? It's the way to be
I'm strange because I'm different
I'll be me
I am lost but I can be forgiven
Show me all that you are in
Show me it won't take that far
To realize your dreams can come true
And they will love you
It's all that they can do
You can be genuine
Without being a bullshit artist
It's ok; you can start now
I was so silly and naive
I'm here to stay - I won't leave

"I'll Sing I'll Dance"

For years you've been on my mind
And I wondered if I was your kind
So I'll take that chance
I'll sing! I'll shout! I'll dance
If you take - take it right now
So I'll show you - I'll show you how
You may run away
Oh, you will bow
Maybe you will stay
I'll take that chance
You may run away
I'll take that chance
Maybe you'll stay
I'll take that chance
You may run away
I don't even know you
But I won't run away
I don't even know you
You won't run away
So I'll tell you my story
And I can show you all my glory
How destiny can play out my part
I'll show you right from the start
Right now I'll show you how
From my heart right now
So please if I tell you
All in advance
I'll tell you
I'll take that chance

“Take That Chance”

I promise I’ll take that chance
I’ll tell you all in advance
I won’t have any doubt
I’ll scream I’ll shout
I’ll show you; I’ll sing I’ll dance
I’ll tell you I’ll give you that chance
I’ll tell you all in advance
I won’t have any doubt
I’ll scream I’ll shout
I’ll tell you like a good friend
I’ll tell you we’ll make amends
I’ll move you like there is no end
I’ll move you and I will send
An angel around a bend
Like no one before like a good friend
Like it’s forever more
I’ll tell you my story
You will sing more
So if you, you let me in
Both of us: we can win

"Misinformed"

When you are misinformed
About something
It's next to nothing
Misinformed about some stupid issue
It's what you will wish
He chose to lie its part
Of human behavior
Now he wonders who will be
His Savior?
When you are misinformed
About something
It's next to nothing
It's what you will wish
It's what you will wish
He chose to lie
It's part of human behavior
When you are misinformed
Who will be his Savior
When you are misinformed
I will scream:
Queen of Sin
Queen of Individuality
King of Nothing

"Pontificate"

Are you pontificating again?
Is this how you win?
You must be really insecure
Or forever more
And two strikes out
Till you'll be
Two strikes out
For you and me
Are you pontificating again?
You stand so tall
But you act like
You hit a brick wall
Are you pontificating again?
Is this how you truly win?
Are you pontificating again
See you have sinned
Is this how you win?
Is this how you win?
Pontificating again
You stand so tall
But you act like
You hit a brick wall
You hit a brick wall
Is this how you win?

"Single Girl"

I push men away
When they want to stay
Why do I do this
Maybe it's a second guess
Is it free will?
I'm climbing up a hill
They say I have
A good sense of intuition
But honestly I do think I will win
I'm a single girl
I push men away
Why do I do this?
Laugh out loud
It's them they want to stay
I push men away
I push men away
When they want to stay
Why do I do this?
When they want to stay
I push men away
I push men away

"Oh, Brother"

Dear Brother: life can take
Those twists and turns
Maybe its so we can learn
You were very mean
Now that it seems
Part of the path I took
I gave it a second look
I am so sorry you were so
Deeply damaged
I could see you could not manage
Growing up- they loved you
Maybe because it's what you do
Brother, when I think of you
And all that what is due
I feel a sense of sadness
It's all part of a big deep mess
I'm so glad we forgave each other
It's because you were my brother
And you were quite cruel
It's ok; you were hurt to

"Strife"

I can be stubborn
A pain in the ass
And wonder how
It will truly last
I am skeptical
One who doubts
Until I find out
What it's all about
You see; it's part of life
Knowing that I was
A strife
It's part of what I have
And how long it will last
I am skeptical
One who doubts
Until I find out
What its all about
I can be stubborn
A pain in the ass
And wonder how
It will truly last

“““I’m Going to Hollywood”

I’m going to Hollywood
I’m going to look real good
I’ll put on couture clothes
No need for pantyhose
I’m going to Hollywood
Gonna shake up that town
Put some light on it
Spread it all around
I see my star on the
Walk of fame
Appreciate their stories
Don’t we all carry shame?
I’m going to Hollywood
I’m gonna look real good
Gonna shake up that town
Spread it all around
I see my star on the
Walk of fame
Appreciate their stories
Don’t we all carry shame?
I’m going to Hollywood
Gonna wish on a star
In the galaxy
Till it fades away
Fade away- fame

"Laughter is timeless. Imagination has no age. And dreams are forever."

–Walt Disney

Printed in the United States
by Baker & Taylor Publisher Services

Printed in the United States
by Baker & Taylor Publisher Services